COMPUTING FOR KIDS

NETWORKS AND THE INTERNET

NANCY DICKMANN

Please visit our website, www.garethstevens.com.
For a free color catalog of all our high-quality books,
call toll free 1-800-542-2595 or fax 1-877-542-2596.

Cataloging-in-Publication Data

Names: Dickmann, Nancy.
Title: Networks and the internet / Nancy Dickmann.
Description: New York : Gareth Stevens Publishing, 2020. | Series: Computing for kids |
Includes glossary and index.
Identifiers: ISBN 9781538252611 (pbk.) | ISBN 9781538252628 (library bound)
Subjects: LCSH: Computer networks--Juvenile literature. | Internet--Juvenile literature.
Classification: LCC TK5105.5 D49 2020 | DDC 004.6--dc23

Published in 2020 by
Gareth Stevens Publishing
111 East 14th Street, Suite 349
New York, NY 10003

For Brown Bear Books Ltd:
Text and Editor: Nancy Dickmann
Children's Publisher: Anne O'Daly
Design Manager: Keith Davis
Designer and illustrator: Supriya Sahai
Picture Manager: Sophie Mortimer
Concept development: Square and Circus

Printed in the United States of America

CPSIA compliance information: Batch #CS20GS: For further information contact Gareth Stevens, New York, New York at 1-800-542-2595.

Picture credits: Front Cover: Shutterstock; Interior: NASA: 12; Shutterstock: anutin 6, ashakyu 10, Casezy Idea 8, dotshock 16, 29b, Fizkes 18, ESB Professional 11, 29t, Lescek Glasner 22, Antonio Guillem 23, Inspiration 15, Gail Johnson 13, JoridC 21, Grunvalds Kaspars 14, 28, KTS Design 25, lightpoet 5, PixieMe 7, Rawpixel.com 9, 19, 20, George Rudy 4, 24, Syda Productions 17, WaveBreakMedia 27, Kerkez Zivka 26.
b=bottom, t=top

Words in the glossary appear in bold type the first time they are used in the text.

CONTENTS

01

CONNECTING COMPUTERS

Computers are very useful. They can do even more when they work together!

You can use smartphones, tablets, and computers to share information.

A computer lets you create and store information. Photos, diary entries, reports, and videos are all types of **data** that a computer can store. But what if you want to share one of these **files** with a friend?

Pass it on!

You could let your friend look at a photo on your computer. But it is easier to send it to her computer. Then she can look at it whenever she likes! Using computers, we share many different types of files every day.

Posting something on the internet is one way of sharing.

Doctors use computers to share information about their patients.

WHAT IS A NETWORK?

A network is a group of linked computers that can work together.

Networks can be large or small. A school might set up a network for the computers that its students use. A big company might set up a bigger network for all the people that work there. Some very large computer networks span the globe.

Computers in a network can share files. They can also use the same printer.

Any device that connects to the internet needs an **IP address,** even a baby monitor.

"IP" is short for "internet protocol."

What's your address?

Each computer in a network needs an "address." This way, other computers in the network can identify it and send it information. A computer address is called an IP address. It is made up of a string of numbers and letters separated by periods.

TYPES OF NETWORKS

Computer networks come in all shapes and sizes.

The simplest type of network is a Personal Area Network (PAN). You might have one in your home. Phones, tablets, laptops, and printers can connect to a PAN. A device called a **router** lets them all connect. All the devices share the same IP address.

Without a router, the devices in your home can't connect with each other.

Wider networks

A Local Area Network (LAN) connects computers across short distances. The computers must be in the same building or a nearby building. To connect computers that are farther apart, you need a Wide Area Network (WAN). A company with offices in two different cities can connect them using a WAN.

A tool called a modem allows a network to communicate with the internet.

The screens at an airport that show information about flights are connected to a network.

SENDING SIGNALS

How do signals travel from one computer in a network to another?

Computers in small networks are often connected by ethernet **cables**. The cables have thin strands of copper wire inside them. Electrical signals travel down the strands. The signals travel very quickly. Plastic coating protects the delicate wires.

All ethernet cables have the same type of connector at the end. It can plug into any computer.

Going wireless

Some networks don't use wires or cables. They send signals using **radio waves**. These invisible waves travel through the air. A **wireless** router sends out a signal that reaches about 100 feet (30 meters). Any device within range can pick it up.

Any device that connects to a network is called a "node."

With a wireless network, you can carry a laptop from one room to another without losing the signal.

THE INTERNET

The biggest computer network stretches across the entire world! We call it the internet.

Billions of people around the world use the internet. Devices can connect to it by cable or wireless. They can also use signals from cell phone towers and even from **satellites** in space. Companies called Internet Service Providers (ISPs) connect networks to the internet.

The internet reaches into space! Astronauts on the International Space Station can connect to it.

Ships lay cables on the ocean floor to connect computers on different continents.

Following the rules

For computers around the world to talk to each other, they need to follow the same rules. For example, **website** addresses must be in a certain format. The same goes for email addresses. These sets of rules are called protocols. All computers that connect to the internet must follow the protocols.

Sharks sometimes damage undersea internet cables by chewing on them!

WHAT IS A WEBSITE?

When we talk about "surfing the internet," we are talking about visiting different websites.

A website is a group of linked pages that you can access through the internet. Some websites provide news or information, such as a weather forecast. Some let you buy or sell things or share photos. Others let you reserve tickets for concerts, movies, or flights.

Many websites follow the same format, with a title banner at the top.

On the page

When you visit a website, the first page you see is called the home page. There may be many other pages linked to it. Menus on the home page can help you find the right page. It is like using a table of contents or an index to find information in a book.

You need a computer program called a browser to connect to a website.

People use HTML, a computer language, to create websites.

SERVERS

You can visit websites from around the world. But where are they actually stored?

The files that make a website are stored on a special computer. It is called a web **server**. No matter where it is, any other computer can connect to it over the internet. The web server may be next door or even in a different country.

Racks of web servers are often kept in buildings called server farms.

Sending a request

When you type a website address into your browser, a server matches it to an IP address. Your browser connects to the server at that IP address. It sends a request for the file that you want. The server sends the file, and it appears on your screen—all in about a second!

A server provides a service to other computers, which are called clients.

A network of web servers lets you access information from anywhere in the world.

SENDING EMAIL

If you want to send a message to a friend, why not use email?

Email is a quick and easy way to keep in touch with family and friends.

We used to write letters on paper and send them through the mail. It could take days or weeks for them to be delivered. Now we can type an email and press "send." The message will be delivered in seconds—even if it has to go around the world!

An email program keeps your messages organized.

Email addresses

An email address has a username and a domain name, separated by the "@" symbol. Many different addresses can share the same domain name. The domain name is like an apartment building, and each username is an individual apartment.

Emails are made up of text, but you can attach photos or other files.

01

MOBILE NETWORKS

With the internet and a smartphone, you can check emails and weather forecasts on the go.

A mobile network lets you send and receive emails, visit websites, and share videos.

Not so long ago, you needed a computer at home or work to access the internet. Now it's much easier! Smartphones, tablets, and some laptops can connect to the internet wherever they are. They use the same wireless system as cell phones.

Cell phone towers are a common sight in cities and towns.

Send and receive

A mobile network is made up of towers that can send and receive signals. When you make a call, your phone signal is picked up by the nearest tower. It sends it to the tower nearest the person you are calling. The towers can send other types of data in the same way.

In a mobile network, signals travel through the air as radio waves.

CLOUD COMPUTING

Wouldn't it be great if you could look up a file from anywhere? Well, now you can!

Many homes have several devices. They can all access the same files, using the cloud.

Say that a person writes a letter on their laptop in the morning. They want to look at it again later. But they only have their phone with them, not their laptop. This is no problem, thanks to the "cloud."

Up in the clouds

In regular computing, files and programs are stored on your computer's **hard disk**. In cloud computing, they are stored on servers connected to the internet. You can access them from any device, no matter where you are.

Files stored in the cloud are safe, even if your computer gets damaged.

You can listen to music files stored in the cloud wherever you are, as long as you're connected to the internet.

HACKERS AND VIRUSES

Computer networks are very useful, but they do also have risks.

If your computer is connected to the internet, it can download dangerous programs called viruses. A virus can damage your computer. A virus might come in a suspicious email, or you might download it by clicking on a link by mistake.

A virus gets inside your body and makes you ill. A **computer virus** gets inside your computer and causes damage.

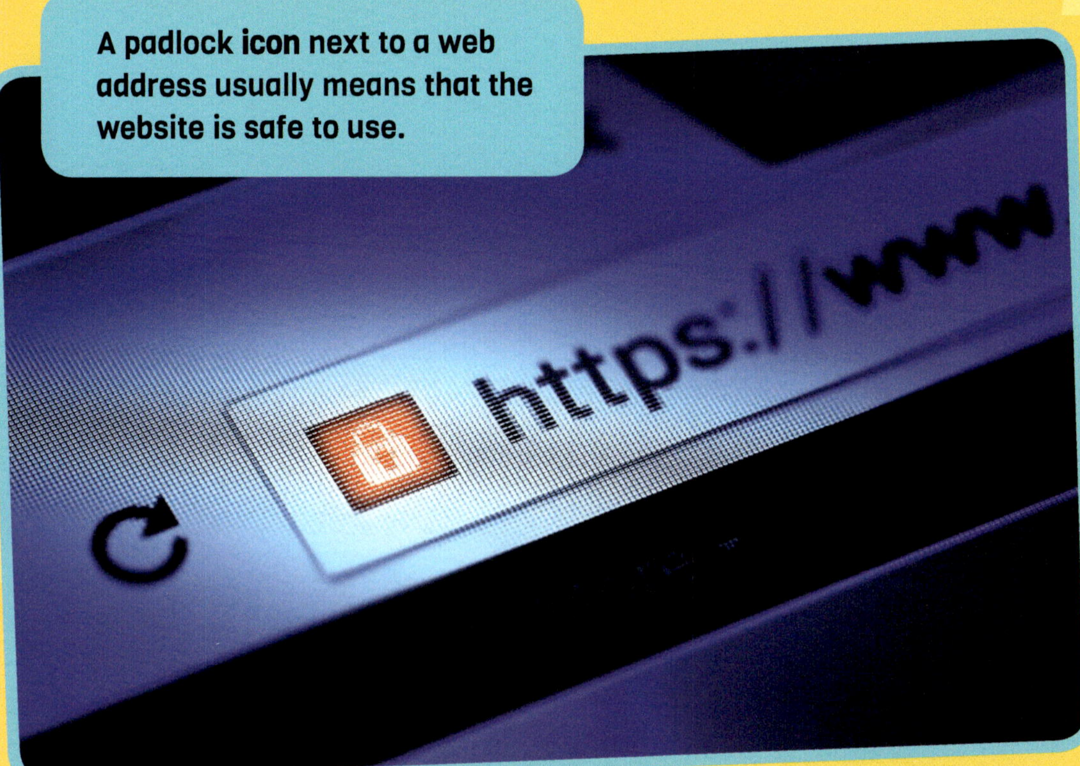

A padlock icon next to a web address usually means that the website is safe to use.

Breaking in

Some criminals use the internet to try to break in to computer networks. They want to steal information, such as bank or credit card details. These people are called hackers. Computer and internet companies work hard to make their networks secure, so hackers can't break in.

A "firewall" is a program that blocks people getting into a computer network.

01 { }

ONLINE SAFETY

A parent or responsible adult should always know what websites you are visiting.

Do you know how to stay safe when you're using the internet?

The internet is an amazing thing. It lets you connect with people from all over the world. But some people aren't who they claim to be. You should never give out your full name or address. You shouldn't arrange to meet up with someone you met online.

Protecting your data

Your computer and your files also need protecting. Delete emails from people or companies that you don't know. Don't click on links or open files unless you trust the person who sent them.

Junk email is called spam. Most of it is just annoying, but some can be dangerous.

If you're ever worried about something that happens online, ask a trusted adult for help.

QUIZ

Try this quiz and test your knowledge of networks and the internet! The answers are on page 32.

1. What is a network?

a. a tool for catching butterflies

b. a group of computers that are linked together

c. a website for sharing photos

2. What does "IP" stand for?

a. Internet Protocol

b. International Police

c. Invisible Pineapple

3. What are menus on a website home page used for?

a. they help you choose what network to connect to

b. they help you find the right web page on the site

c. they help you decide what to have for supper

4. What is a web server?

a. a type of South American spider

b. a cable that connects two computers

c. a powerful computer that stores websites

5. What is the last part of an email address called?

a. a domain name

b. a username

c. a nickname

6. How do signals travel in a mobile network?

a. on the backs of tiny flies

b. as invisible radio waves

c. through copper wires

7. How can you keep your photos and music files in the cloud?

a. store them on a server that's connected to the internet

b. store them on a mobile phone

c. attach them to a balloon and let them float into the sky

8. What does a hacker do?

a. helps set up your home network

b. sneaks into an office building to steal computers

c. tries to break into computer networks to steal information

GLOSSARY

browser a computer program used for accessing and interacting with websites

cable a wire or bundle of wires with a protective casing, used for transmitting electrical signals

computer language a language that is used in programming computers

computer virus a computer program that can damage a computer that downloads it

data information that is stored or used in a computer, in the form of a series of ones and zeroes

file data, such as a report or a digital photo, that is stored on a computer's hard disk

hard disk the part of a computer where files and programs are stored

icon a symbol that represents a computer application on a screen

internet a huge computer network that connects computers all over the world

IP address a unique string of numbers and letters that identifies each computer using a network

program a set of coded instructions for a computer to follow

radio waves invisible waves of energy that travel through the air and can be used to send information

router an electrical device that forwards information and signals to the different computers in a network

satellite an artificial object sent into orbit around Earth, which can send and receive communication signals

server a computer that stores and sends out information to other computers

website a group of linked web pages

wireless a way of connecting to a network using radio waves instead of wires

FIND OUT MORE

Books

Gifford, Clive. *Computer Networks (Get Connected to Digital Literacy).* New York: Crabtree Publishing Company, 2015.

Mapua, Jeff. *Networks (Let's Learn About Computer Science).* Berkeley Heights, NJ: Enslow Publishing, 2019.

Reed, Jennifer. *What Are Computer Networks and the Internet? (Let's Find Out!).* New York: Rosen Publishing, 2018.

Rooney, Anne. *You Wouldn't Want to Live Without the Internet!* New York: Franklin Watts, 2015.

Websites

Go here to find answers to questions about computers:
www.bbc.com/bitesize/subjects/zyhbwmn

Check out this map to see where the world's underwater internet cables are:
submarine-cable-map-2018.telegeography.com

This website will give you more information about computer networks:
www.bbc.com/bitesize/guides/zc6rcdm/revision/1

Take this quiz to test your knowledge of online safety:
www.safekids.com/quiz

Publisher's note to educators and parents: Our editors have carefully reviewed these websites to ensure that they are suitable for students. Many websites change frequently, however, and we cannot guarantee that a site's future contents will continue to meet our high standards of quality and educational value. Be advised that students should be closely supervised whenever they access the internet.

INDEX

Quiz answers
1. b; 2. a; 3. b; 4. c; 5. a; 6. b; 7. a; 8. c

COMPUTING FOR KIDS

ISBN: 9781538252611
6-Pack ISBN: 9781538254219
9 781538 252611

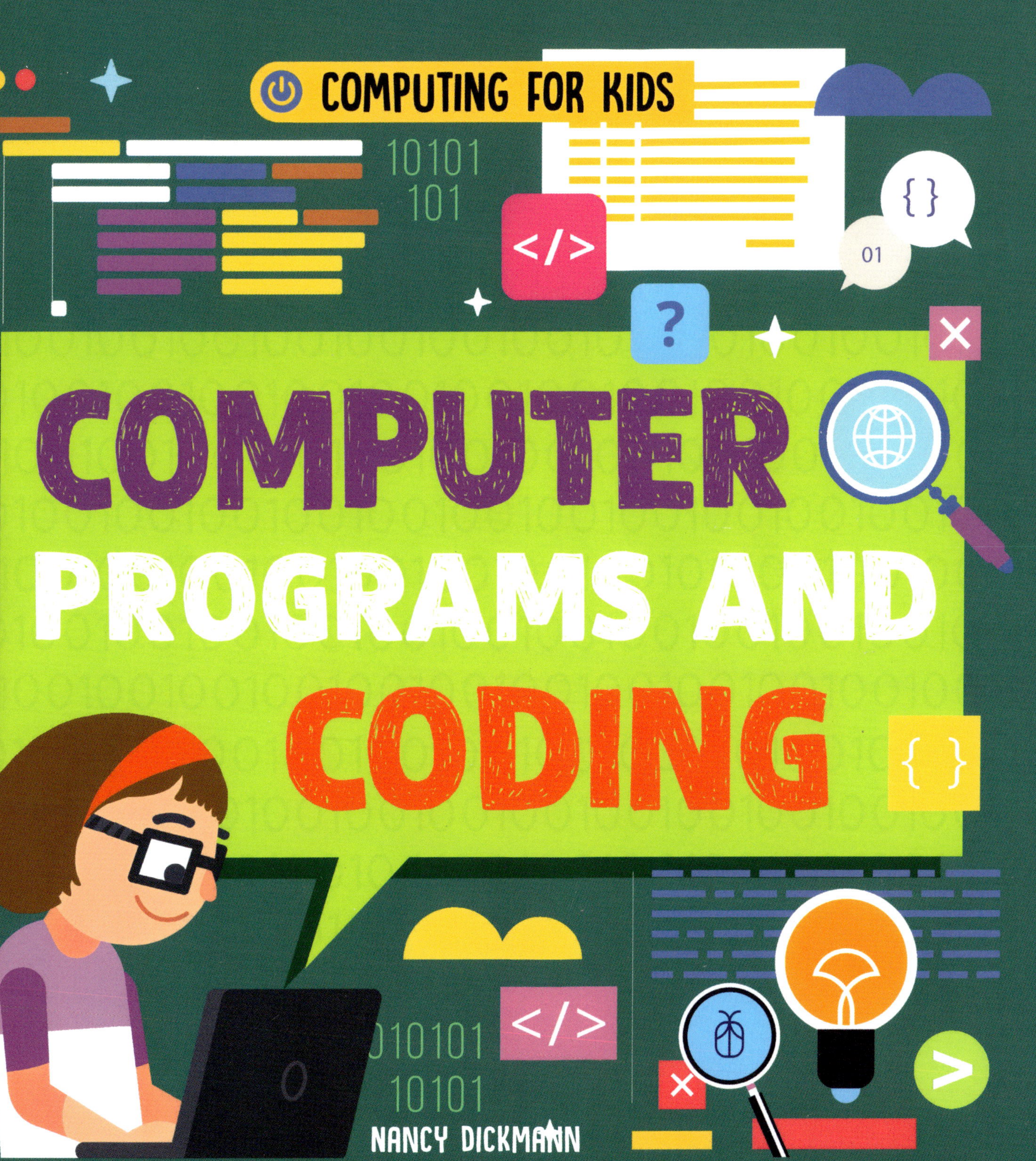
COMPUTING FOR KIDS
COMPUTER PROGRAMS AND CODING
NANCY DICKMANN